Published by Christianityworks

© Berni Dymet
2nd Edition - Published 2015

ISBN: 978-0-9775536-1-7

Scripture verses quoted are taken from
The New International Version

Cover design: Mariah Reilly,
Sydney Australia.

Printed & bounded in India
Kala Jyothi Process Pvt. Ltd.

christianityworks

Berni Dymet

How to Get
Close to

God

christianity**works**

Contents

INTRODUCTION

God yearns jealously for the spirit that he has made to dwell in us... ***Draw near to God and he will draw near to you***...humble yourself before the Lord and he will exalt you. (James 4:5-10)

That I should be the one to write this humble little volume about drawing close to God is such an incredible testimony to God's outrageous grace. Because for me, it all began - this Jesus thing - in a dark and dangerous hour. A time in my life when I was such a long way off from God... at least that's how it seemed.

And yet, it was in the middle of the darkest nights on the stormiest oceans of life that His grace found me. His light shone for me. I shall never forget the inky blackness that surrounded me on those days. And I shall never forget how my Saviour reached out to me in that place.

My prayer for you, as we journey together for a time, is that this little book will be a signpost, a marker that points you Christ-ward. And that as you read the simple, beautiful, and profound truths in these pages, the Spirit of God will write them on your heart, so that you will never be alone again.

Your servant in Christ,

Berni Dymet

QUESTIONS

Not long ago, I was talking with a man in Africa. His country had been living through a bloody conflict that had claimed the lives of many innocent men, women, and children.

He had been serving in the military and I can't imagine the atrocities that he'd seen.

That's why I wasn't shocked when he said to me, "You know, Berni, after everything I've been through, I just can't believe that there is a God. And if there is, He certainly isn't interested in the lives of everyday people like you and me."

It's like that sometimes, isn't it?

We look at the circumstances of our own lives and those of people around the globe, and those circumstances are so powerful, so compelling, that we end up wondering, "Where the blazes is God anyway? Is He interested in my life...really?"

"And if God is God, how can I get close to Him?"

This last one is a question that so many people confront at some point in their lives. They want to believe, but...

So that's the very question that we'll be exploring together in this book - *How can we get close to God?* In fact, let me state it in a slightly different way. *How can you and I get close to God?* Because it's a deeply personal and intimate thing - this relationship between God and each one of us.

How can we get close to Him?

Whether we find ourselves feeling a long way away from God today, or whether it's been an experience in our past, or whether it's a place that we'll pass through sometime in the future, I pray that God will use this book to encourage us, to inspire us, and to show us how we can know Him in an intimate and deeply personal way...each and every day. How we can be closer to God than we ever thought possible. Closer even than the deepest secrets of our hearts.

That, my friend, is my prayer for you and for me today.

CHAPTER ONE

blood relatives

blood relatives

The Boat that Just Drifted Away...

If I look back on my life as a teenager, I had everything - a good home, a good school, great friends. And later in my high school life, I encountered Jesus. I believed in Him and began a relationship with Him. In fact, I committed my life to Him.

You know what it's like when we're teenagers. We have the luxury of innocent idealism and we're not afraid to be dreamers. And for me, as a

JESUS JUST DIDN'T FIT THE REALITIES OF CAREER AND MONEY AND OPPORTUNITY THAT PRESENTED THEMSELVES.

teenager, somehow it was so much easier to believe in Jesus than it was when I grew up into adulthood.

And grow up I did! I had the responsibility and the money and the mortgage and the career and the car…all the things that come with being 'an adult'. And the plain reality of it all was that God was pushed into the back seat. I simply didn't need Him.

Jesus just didn't fit the realities of career and money and opportunity that presented themselves.

I still believed in Him for a while, but little by little I headed off in my own direction. After all, I was grown up! I'd matured. And when that happened it was natural for me to conclude that…well, I didn't need that Jesus stuff anymore.

Our Perception is Our Reality

The longer I allowed that to go on - and it went on for a long time…in fact, a couple of decades - the less real He became. Because reality is about where we're living. We see the world from where we sit.

Our perception *is* our reality.

If we're walking every day with Jesus, praying and enjoying our relationship with Him, then that relationship is real. It's alive. But if we're focusing on all the things in the 'here and now'…if we allow our senses to be filled with the sights and sounds and smells of creation alone…then all too quickly, the Creator fades from our view.

Now that's not just a 'God' thing. It happens in every relationship.

A man and a woman come together in marriage. They love each other and they enjoy each other. But as time drifts by they so often begin to focus on a whole bunch of other things that crowd out the relationship part of their marriage. Work. Career. The kids. Money. Buying and having and possessing.

And eventually, sadly, the two who were meant to be one, drift apart again to become two. Eventually, the marriage fails. You and I know that this is happening in epidemic proportions. "We've just grown apart," they will say.

FOR ANY RELATIONSHIP TO SUCCEED, IT HAS TO BE A BIG PART OF OUR PRESENT REALITY. MAKES SENSE, DOESN'T IT?

For any relationship to succeed, it has to be a big part of our present reality. Makes sense, doesn't it?

9

Well, it's the same thing with God.

A Fading Reality

We can be focused on a whole bunch of other things and still kind of believe in Jesus - still have that 'faith' somewhere in our heads. But the longer we leave it to gather dust on some shelf in our heads, instead of living it with our lives; the longer we focus on other things and not on that relationship with Him, the less real it becomes. The faith fades.

And on top of that, because Jesus is not a physical reality - He's not here in the flesh and blood the way a husband or wife is - then we can come to a point (which is the point I came to in my life) of thinking *"Well, does He still exist at all? Is He real?"*

Right about then it's not unusual for the crowd to fade from view, or for circumstances to take a turn for the worse. Maybe we lose our job, or there's a broken relationship, or we have money worries, or we just don't have a good sense of our own well-being.

And at that point we wonder, "Where's God in all this? Is He real? How can He let this happen? Does He really care about me?"

My hunch is that this is something we all go through in our lives. There's a point at which we feel like God is a million miles away no matter what course our spiritual journey had taken up to that point. "What happened? Where did He go? Why is it like this?"

That's exactly the point at which I found myself in February 1995. My life was falling apart. All the things that had been so important to me up to that point - the shiny baubles of my life, my hopes and dreams - lay shattered at my feet.

> "WHAT HAPPENED?
> WHERE DID HE GO?
> WHY IS IT
> LIKE THIS?"

The best that I could pray in those dark days and weeks and months, the most that I could muster in faith terms was, *"God, if you're real, if you're out there, I need you! Now would be a really good time ... if you exist."* That's all I had, I just didn't know anymore. Because for so long I'd been walking in a different direction.

I'd been living a different reality. I'd been focusing on other things for so long that He wasn't real to me anymore.

Frankly, Jesus was a 'maybe'…where once He'd been 'my Lord'. That's it. That's how it was. And right smack bang in the middle of that little lot, the question was simply, *"What do I have to do to get close to God?"*

11

The Bridge that Spans the Universe

Let me share with you an utterly outrageous statement from a man named Paul, one of the Apostles of Jesus Christ. He wrote this two thousand years ago. And the reason it's so outrageous is that Paul was a Pharisee. He was a religious separatist. He was so much into 'religion through good works', I can't begin to find the words…

And yet after he met Jesus Christ on the road to Damascus, this is what he wrote:

> *But now in Christ Jesus, you who were once far away have been brought near through the blood of Christ… He came and preached peace to you who were far away and peace to those who were near. For through him we both have access to the Father by one Spirit.* (Ephesians 2:13-18)

You who were once far away! You who once thought that God was a million miles away. You who once thought that you had to shout clear across the universe for Him to hear you. You who thought that you had to build a bridge back to Him through your good works.

You have been brought near to Him by the blood of Christ…that bridge of grace that reaches clear across that eternal and unbridgeable divide between God and each one of us.

In other words, the only thing that you and I have to do to be brought near to God is to believe that Jesus died for us. That's what Paul means by "you who were once far away have been brought near by the blood of Christ."

While all our failures, all our wrongs, all of that junk that God calls *'sin'* has a price, that price was paid for by Jesus on the Cross. That's what 'the blood' thing is all about.

In the Hebrew culture, blood was a symbol for life. He paid with His life. He spilt His blood for you and for me…to pay for our sin.

Now, Christians have heard this message so many times it can almost become passé. The more familiar we are with something, the less attention we pay to it - even if it's a deep, life-transforming truth.

The Gospel - *the good news* - well, it can wash past us sometimes and we end up just believing it in our heads. But what about believing it with our hearts and with our very lives? Believing in the fact that Jesus died and rose again to pay for our sins, our wrongs, our junk…whatever label you care to use? And then taking that deep truth and letting it sink in. Drinking it in and soaking it in… so that it becomes a part of who we are.

What about believing it with our lives? Well?

Because when we do, there's peace - peace with God. Hostilities cease, because the separation, the barrier, the obstacle is gone. The unbridgeable divide is bridged in an instant. There's no more distance between Him and you - or Him and me - as there once was between enemies.

> IT'S TIME TO START LIVING OUR LIVES IN THAT OUTRAGEOUS PROMISE!

Peace has broken out. That's the promise! *We who were once far off are brought near by the blood of Christ.* And you know something? It's time to start living our lives in that outrageous promise!

A Different Perspective

If you won millions in the lottery, would that change the way you lived your life?

Well, this is better than winning millions in the lottery! This is more than that. This is believing that we are set free for eternal life that begins here and now. The war is over! Peace has been declared! It may not feel like that, but that's the promise that we can believe in.

There's no more gap. 'Far away' becomes 'near'.

And faith in that promise is *the* starting point of getting close to God. In fact, it's *the only* starting point. We are now blood relatives with Jesus. Adopted into His family. Accepted by His grace. We no longer have to be afraid, that we're a long way off.

> *For you did not receive a spirit that makes you a slave again to fear, but you received the Spirit of sonship. And by him we cry, "Abba, Father." The Spirit himself testifies with our spirit that we are God's children. Now if we are children, then we are heirs – heirs of God and co-heirs with Christ, if indeed we share in his sufferings in order that we may also share in his glory.* (Romans 8:15-17)

Blood relatives, heirs and co-heirs with Christ. Because God made it so through His Son. A bridge that spans eternity. A bridge that spans the universe. A bridge called *grace*.

That is where it all begins. With God's grace. And everything...*everything* needed to open the door to that relationship has already been done for us by Jesus on that Cross.

However uncertain we may feel...however feeble our faith may at first appear...however dark the hour may be, we *are* brought near to God by the blood of Christ.

We discover that whilst we had wandered 'far away', that through Christ, God is closer than we could ever have imagined. That's the startling paradox of grace.

> THAT IS WHERE IT ALL BEGINS. WITH GOD'S GRACE.

All we need to do, you and I, is to believe.

The simple truth…the good news that you and I will ever need…is that when we put our complete trust in what Jesus did for each one of us on that Cross - the price that He paid for our sin with His life - *we are brought near to God.*

Grace is as simple as it is beautiful.

CHAPTER TWO

God sets up home

CHAPTER TWO

God sets up home

After the First Step...

In the last chapter we looked at God's promise...that if we believe that Jesus died for our sins, then we are brought close to Him. That promise is kind of like the marriage promise that a husband and wife make at their wedding. It's completely unconditional. It's a promise for life. And from God's perspective, there is no divorce.

He will never break it. It's a promise that we can live our lives in...with absolute certainty!

So, the first step that brings us close to God...is the step that He takes through the Cross towards us. It's a step that He takes towards *each one of us*. The Cross is for you and for me. The Cross opens the way to God - for

each one of us. In fact, the Cross *is* the Way.

And the only response He requires of us is simply to believe in Him with all that we are. With our very lives. To put our faith in Jesus.

> SO OFTEN, I'VE SAT QUIETLY ON MY OWN, JUST GAZING WITH THE EYES OF MY SOUL AT THE WONDROUS CROSS, AND WEPT WITH JOY.

I don't know about you, but every time I rest in that wondrous truth, my heart is fit to burst with a joy that I can't describe. So often, I've sat quietly on my own, just gazing with the eyes of my soul at the wondrous Cross, and wept with joy at God's incomprehensible plan to draw me close to Him.

Those times are without doubt the high points of my life - even if all around there are dark storm clouds…as there often are in life.

Now, in this chapter I want to look at the next step to getting close to God. He took the first mighty step, we responded with a small stumble of faith, and there it is - the marriage promise. The eternal relationship between God and you…between God and me…has begun. An eternal marriage.

But what comes next? How do we experience the closeness…the intimacy of that relationship in the reality of our lives?

Weddings are Wonderful, but…

…they don't go on forever. They're celebrations… when everybody gets dressed up. Family and friends come along. And there's a beautiful ceremony where a man and woman decide, in front of everybody, to make that promise. That declaration that they are going to spend the rest of their lives together. Then they have the ceremony. They sign the register. There are flowers and photos and a feast…it's just fabulous!

And it's exactly the same at that moment when we go to God and ask for His forgiveness and accept Jesus Christ as our Saviour and Lord. That's an awesome, awesome thing! If it's something you've never done, I just want to encourage you…that there's no time like right now to pray just a simple prayer.

I remember back to our own wedding, when Jacqui and I were married. It's a few years ago now, but it was just unreal. Being a typical male, I said, "Well, why don't we just go to church on Sunday morning and have the wedding as part of the Sunday service… and we can have coffee and fairy bread afterwards."

Not surprisingly, Jacqui didn't quite see it that way! Instead, we hired a white marquee and put it up on the vacant block next to the church building, and our friends and family came along. (By the way, I still had fairy bread served up to her at the bridal table. And I have the video with the priceless look of utter horror on her face when the plate arrived!)

THE BEST PART OF THAT DAY FOR ME WAS WHEN WE LEFT EVERYBODY ELSE BEHIND.

Anyway, it was just a wonderful celebration of a man and a woman falling in love and deciding to spend the rest of their lives together as husband and wife.

But you know, the best part of that day for me was when, at the end of the celebration, the car came to pick us up…and we left everybody else behind. I still remember that feeling when we hopped into the car that we'd hired to take us to the airport…so that we could fly off on our honeymoon. I remember waving to the people and driving off thinking, "This is by far the best part of the wedding…leaving the people behind!"

It's not so much that I didn't enjoy the celebration. That was great. But heading off together as husband

and wife was awesome. And so began that process of becoming one, of making a life together and a home together.

And it's exactly the same when we leave the rest of the world behind for Christ's sake. When we accept Jesus into our hearts. When we accept once and for all His offer of an eternal relationship through His sacrifice on the Cross.

What is it that happens next after that beautiful 'marriage' promise?

Exactly the same as in a marriage. We set up house together. We move in with one another - God moves into us…and we move into Him. We live together with God…as one.

That's Jesus' plan. Take a look:

> *"If you love me, you will obey what I command. And I will ask the Father, and he will give you another Counselor to be with you forever – the Spirit of truth. The world cannot accept him, because it neither sees him nor knows him. But you know him, **for he lives with you and will be in you.** I will not leave you as orphans; I will come to you. Before long, the world will not see me anymore, but you will see me. Because I live,*

you also will live. On that day you will realise that I am in my Father, and you are in me, and I am in you. Whoever has my commands and obeys them, he is the one who loves me. He who loves me will be loved by my Father, and I too will love him and show myself to him."

Then Judas (not Judas Iscariot) said, "But, Lord, why do you intend to show yourself to us and not to the world?"

*Jesus replied, "If anyone loves me, he will obey my teaching. My Father will love him, **and we will come to him and make our home with him.** He who does not love me will not obey my teaching. These words you hear are not my own; they belong to the Father who sent me".* (John 14:15-23)

Under One Roof

That, my friend, is the language of intimacy and closeness…and eternal living with God.

And isn't that what it means to be close? I couldn't imagine living apart from my wife Jacqui. In fact, just as I write these words, I'm sitting in an airport lounge, about to head off overseas and be apart from her for a week and a half.

24

I love being about God's business but this travelling thing is always such a sacrifice for me…because I hate being away from Jacqui. And even before I step onto that plane, I'm sitting here thinking about being back with her. That's what marriage is.

Why would we imagine that it's any different in our relationship with God?

Imagine going to a wedding - a great celebration - but afterwards, instead of the bride and groom heading off to make their lives together under the one roof, the husband goes back to *his* old home and the wife goes back to *her* old home.

> THEY HAVE THE CELEBRATION, BUT THEY NEVER MAKE A HOME TOGETHER! THEY NEVER LIVE OUT THE PROMISE WITH THEIR LIVES.

They make the promises, they have the celebration, but they never make a home together! They never live out the promise with their lives.

Now, we have some friends who were married recently. He's an Australian and she's from the Philippines. And because of the immigration laws in Australia, she was forced to leave the country after the wedding. And for several months - until it was all sorted out - they had to live apart, even though they were married.

They were devastated. It was the most awful time for them. But you know something? That's how some people approach their relationship with God.

And that's the very reason that so many people believe in Jesus and yet never experience the intimacy - the utter one-ness with Him - that comes from living their lives with Him.

The Price of Intimacy

I want you to notice that when Jesus spoke of this intimacy, He put clear conditions on it. Let's look at it again (this time as an abridged version):

> *"If you love me, you will obey what I command...* Because I live, you also will live. On that day you will realise that I am in my Father, and you are in me, and I am in you. *Whoever has my commands and obeys them, he is the one who loves me. He who loves me will be loved by my Father, and I too will love him and show myself to him...*
>
> *"If anyone loves me, he will obey my teaching. My Father will love him,* and we will come to him and make our home with him. He who does not love me

will not obey my teaching. These words you hear are not my own; they belong to the Father who sent me."
(John 14:15-23)

There is clearly a price to pay for this intimacy. Just as there is a price to pay for being married. Now it's so easy to dismiss this. For instance, someone might say, "You see, I knew that when it comes right down to it, religion is just a bunch of rules."

"YOU SEE, I KNEW THAT WHEN IT COMES RIGHT DOWN TO IT, RELIGION IS JUST A BUNCH OF RULES".

The same could be said of the constraints that marriage places on us. Before I married Jacqui I was free to come and go as I please. I was free to date other women. But, when I married this wonderful woman that God gave me, I had to give up those 'freedoms'.

Since marrying Jacqui, I just can't decide to go out every night with my friends, because I have a wife to consider. And I definitely can't go out with other women (obviously!). Yet far from feeling restricted in those natural 'constraints' that come with the exclusivity of marriage, the exact opposite is true. Yes, perhaps we can see them as sacrifices. But they are the very things that set me free to experience the wondrous intimacy that only marriage brings.

So many of us, when we accept Christ, say, "Yippee! Isn't this wonderful!"

But then we go on and live life as though nothing has changed. As though believing in Jesus isn't a new life. It's as crazy a notion as a man and a woman getting married and going back to their old lives and living in separate houses and dating other people! And then we wonder, "Well, why is it that I'm not experiencing the closeness to Jesus that other people seem to have?"

When you love someone and you've made that life-long promise of exclusive commitment, setting up home together is wonderful. But yes, it's an adjustment and it involves sacrifice. And anyone who's been married for any length of time will tell you that it's not easy some days. But it's God's plan. Not only for a husband and wife, but for each one of us when we believe in Jesus Christ.

And when a man forsakes relationships with other women for his wife, and when she forsakes relationships with other men for her husband - that is, as you and I plainly know, the place of beautiful intimacy. It's the closest human relationship possible.

Listen again to what Jesus says:

> *"Those who love me will keep my word and my Father will love them and we will come to them and make our home in them."* (John 14:23)

Isn't that outrageous?!

Isn't that so different from the notion that you can believe in God - you can believe in Jesus - and still keep Him at a distance? It's a beautiful picture of Jesus saying, "If you love me, we're going to come and make our home in you."

Father, Son, Holy Spirit…indwelling us because we've taken the step of faith.

An Incredible Invasion

A few years ago I was talking with a young Jewish lawyer about this very question, and he said to me, "Hang on just a minute! Isn't that an incredible invasion of privacy?" I was stunned, I'd never looked at it that way. It still brings a smile to my face today.

Yep. I guess living together is a bit of an invasion of privacy. But when you love each other, you want to be together. And you want to pay the price. There's not a single part of me that wants to have a relationship with any other woman other than Jacqui.

And it's the same in my relationship with God. Yes, I make mistakes. I make mistakes every day. Because I'm human. But then I look at the obedience that Jesus calls me to…(Actually, there are very, very few things that He says to us. "Don't do!") And, when I look at those - like stealing, slandering, arguing, lying - it is blindingly obvious that they're the selfish things that ruin our lives anyway!

The full effect of what Jesus is saying here runs something like this:

> *If you love me, I'll come and live with you. I'll never leave you. Everywhere you go, every minute of every day, I will be with you.*

GOD'S ADDRESS ON PLANET EARTH IS YOU, IF YOU BELIEVE IN JESUS CHRIST.

That's the second part of God's promise…that He will come and make His home in us. God's address on planet earth is me. God's address on planet earth is you… if you believe in Jesus Christ. And He will never, never move out.

The marriage vow - the first part - is the grace of the Cross, and our heartfelt response of "I believe!"

But I don't love my wife with my head, I love my wife

with my heart and with my life. And in the same way, I don't love my God with my head, I love my God with my heart and with my life. And because it's a heart relationship, the next logical step is that we should live together in a home, in a close personal relationship that's real…and that is the promise of God.

It's a promise of eternal intimacy open to each person who believes, and who sets their heart to accept God on His terms through simple, faithful obedience.

A Simple Decision

I know that some days, when I make mistakes - when I *sin* - it disrupts my intimacy with God. It feels as though my prayer is just bouncing off the ceiling. Just as intimacy in a marriage is disrupted when husband and wife argue. That's why I keep a short account with my God. That's why I go to Him as quickly as I can…to say sorry, to seek His forgiveness, to turn away (to turn away means to repent) from what I know to be wrong.

And my God forgives me every time. Because that sin is already paid for on the Cross by Jesus. In fact, He forgives in an instant. And that forgiveness is what restores the fellowship between us and Him - the closeness…the intimacy.

This is where God makes the rubber hit the road. You may feel like He's a million miles away, but when that happens, we can fall back on the promises of God. Those two promises are…that He has brought us close to Him through the blood of his Son…and that He has made His home in us.

Those are God's unbreakable promises that He will not change.

> WILL WE STEP INTO THE PARADOX OF THE FREEDOM OF LIFE IN CHRIST, BY OBEDIENCE TO HIM?

Now, we have a decision to make. The same decision that a man and a woman make as the foundation of marriage. Will we - you and I - serve Him and Him alone? Will we obey Him? Will we accept His ways above our ways…above the world's seductive comforts and creeds?

Will we step into the paradox of the freedom of life in Christ, by obedience to Him?

Because - let me say this plainly - until our hearts and our lives cry out with a resounding "YES!"… that intimacy with God, that closeness that our heart desires, will forever elude us.

The decision is yours. The decision is mine. It's such a simple decision. And yet so many tarry on the fringes of a relationship with God… because of what it may cost them.

Let me share with you some beautiful words from A W Tozer's book, *The Pursuit of God*. Because these words may just help a soul here or there finally… finally cry out that all-important "YES!" with their very lives:

UNTIL OUR HEARTS AND OUR LIVES CRY OUT WITH A RESOUNDING YES! THAT INTIMACY WITH GOD, THAT CLOSENESS THAT OUR HEART DESIRES, WILL FOREVER ELUDE US.

The man who has God for his treasure has all things in One. Many ordinary treasures may be denied him, or if he is allowed to have them, the enjoyment of them will be so tempered that they will never be necessary to his happiness. Or if he must see them go, one after one, he will scarcely feel a sense of loss, for having the Source of all things he has in One all satisfaction, all pleasure, all delight. Whatever he may lose he has actually lost nothing, for he now has it all in One, and he has it purely, legitimately and forever.

33

CHAPTER THREE

amidst the cut and thrust of life

amidst the cut and thrust of life

Real Life

For most people these days, life is pretty hectic. Family, work, mobile phones, email, taking the kids here and running them there… Somehow, we seem to be working longer and playing less.

And while life can be filled with possibilities and opportunities, some days there are tensions and stresses. There just are. And somewhere in the middle of all that, we can get to wondering, "Where's God today? I wonder if he's going to show up!"

But it's only a fleeting thought, because we're so busy. Running late at work again, we wonder, "Will I make it in time to take the kids to football practice?" Our minds are focused on the *stuff* that we're involved in. Right here and right now.

Then you get to the end of the day and you feel drained. You wonder, "Why didn't God show up today? What's the matter with me? Isn't He interested? What do I have to do to get close to God?"

Ever been there? I have. In fact, I used to be there almost every day. And when that's the reality of our lives, we can get to thinking, "Well, that's just the way it is." We accept this distant, fleeting, every-now-and-then relationship with God…forgetting completely the words that Jesus prayed for you and me just before He was crucified.

Words that tell us what lay behind His decision to take the road of crucifixion:

> *"My prayer is not for them alone. I pray also for those who will believe in me through their message* [that's you and me], *that all of them may be one, Father, just as you are in me and I am in you. May they also be in us so that the world may believe that you have sent me. I have given them the glory that you gave me, that they may be one as we are one: I in them and you in me. May they be brought to complete unity to let the world*

*know that you sent me and have loved them even as
you have loved me. Father, I want those you have given
me to be with me where I am, and to see my glory, the
glory you have given me because you loved me before
the creation of the world." (John 17:20-24)*

And that is why Jesus went to the Cross. So that He
could be one with you and me. Can there be any greater
love than that?

But then there's just
the hectic reality of life,
isn't there? And then that
prayer that Jesus prayed
for you and for me in
those dark hours seems
just such an incredibly
long way off!

> AND THAT IS WHY
> JESUS WENT TO THE
> CROSS. SO THAT
> HE COULD BE ONE
> WITH YOU AND ME.

Perhaps you're a mother and you're changing
dirty nappies…and your child has nappy rash and she's
teething and you haven't had sleep and you're wondering,
"Whatever happened to being able to go to work?
Whatever happened to intelligent adult conversation?"
And you feel like your world's falling apart.

Let me ask you something - Is God in that place
with you?

Or maybe you're at work and you go to a tough meeting. The politics is running rife. You're under threat. And you're so tense you could cut the air with a knife. You're tired. You're threatened. You're at risk.

Let me ask you something - Is God in that place with you?

Whatever your place and circumstances and routine is today and tomorrow and the next day...do you believe that Jesus is God in that place with you?

A Tragic Choice

This is a conundrum that everyone who sets their hearts on following Christ will face at some point. We can step out and believe in Jesus. We can decide that we're going to bow every part of our lives down to Him. But then...then life just gets busy. Very busy. And we have an amazing propensity to focus on the here and now. The things that we have to deal with today.

And all that Jesus stuff...well, that has to wait. Somehow we separate our walk with Jesus from our walk through life. We Westerners in particular are very good at that - spirituality in one box, life in the other. Jesus over there and life over here.

And so we don't experience that intimacy, that

closeness with the One whom we call Lord. It frustrates the living daylights out of us. And before we know it, we're saying, "Aaahhh! It's just all too hard!"

We just acquiesce. We accept this poverty of relationship as the normative Christian life. What an utter tragedy!

WE ACCEPT THIS POVERTY OF RELATIONSHIP AS THE NORMATIVE CHRISTIAN LIFE. WHAT AN UTTER TRAGEDY!

Put yourself in Jesus' shoes for a moment in that time leading up to His crucifixion. Knowing what was going to happen. The ache in His heart. And that heartfelt prayer…

> *"Father, I want those you have given me to be with me where I am, and to see my glory, the glory you have given me because you loved me before the creation of the world."* (John 17:24)

And then He went to the Cross for you and me. How can we make such a tragic mistake? What is the answer? How do we solve this dilemma?

The Thing That Pleases God Most

> *Without faith it is impossible to please God, because anyone who comes to him must believe that he exists*

41

and that he rewards those who earnestly seek him.
(Hebrews 11:6)

Believe and seek. Believe that He is here. Believe that
He will do what He says He will do. And seek Him with
all our hearts. Earnestly.

To tell you the truth, in the early days I felt a little silly
earnestly seeking after someone I couldn't see.

Yet God placed a desire, a yearning in my heart that
couldn't be satisfied by anyone but God Himself. And
when I finally surrendered all to Him, when finally I laid
down my life for Him, He filled me with His Presence.
The Spirit of God, just as Jesus promised. With a joy
unspeakable.

And well meaning friends said to me, "Berni, it won't
always be like this. You won't always experience the sort
of joy that you're feeling now." I recall being told that
one day and going home…angry. I said to God, "Lord,
if I can't have this joy forever, then I don't want this
Christianity thing. If I can't know you intimately all the
time, then what's the point?"

Sure, there have been tough times along the way.
Absolutely there have. But this 'sophisticated' man of the
world - this businessman who'd been clawing his way to

the top - just decided to believe the promises that Jesus
made, like a little child. And since that time, I have lived
my life in the joy of the Lord. A joy unspeakable.
A wondrous, intimate relationship with Jesus Christ.

Do you feel that desire, that yearning in your heart
today? I believe that that's exactly why we're here
together in this book right now. Because He wants to
fan the flame of your desire for Him today.

This is not some
complex proposition.
Sometimes we complicate
things too much. Jesus
promised to save us from
our mess (sin) with an

> DO YOU FEEL
> THAT DESIRE, THAT
> YEARNING IN YOUR
> HEART TODAY?

eternal life that is all about having an intimate closeness
with Him. We receive that by believing in what He
did for us on the Cross. And along with that, He also
promises us a new life, because the former without the
latter doesn't make sense. He promised us the Holy
Spirit. He promised us an incredibly intimate oneness
with Him. He promised to dwell in us…to make His
home in us.

And we make it so complicated.

Jesus said, "I praise you, Father, Lord of heaven and earth, because you have hidden these things from the wise and learned, and revealed them to little children. Yes, Father, for this was your good pleasure." (Matthew 11:25-26)

Wake up! It's time to believe that this relationship - this beautiful closeness with God - is for us. Right here and right now.

> IT'S NOT ENOUGH JUST TO BELIEVE GOD'S PROMISES FROM A DISTANCE. THERE CAN BE NO CLOSENESS AT A DISTANCE.

That's what it means to live our lives in the promises of God. That's what we talked about in the first two chapters of this book.

Let me be very plain and direct at this point. It's not enough just to believe God's promises from a distance. There can be no closeness at a distance, any more than there can be intimacy between a husband and a wife who live under separate roofs. God wants us to believe in His promises right in the middle of our daily lives. He wants us to believe His promise to be with us and to make His home with us. He wants us to believe that right now...in every circumstance that we walk through in life.

Whether good, bad, beautiful, or ugly…Jesus is there in that place with you, just as He is with me.

And the thing that pleases God most is when we put our faith in Him and His promises (the two are inseparable because God and His Word are one).

Let's Get Real

In my life I'm basically involved in full-time ministry doing what I'm doing right now here with you. But I also still do a bit of Information Technology consulting work (that's the background I've come from).

Some of the organisations that I work with can be tough places…where the pressure is on. I can be sitting in a meeting in some big boardroom looking

WE CAN BE CLOSE WHEN WE'RE APART.

out over Sydney Harbour and the city. You press the button on the wall and they bring in the coffee. There are $2 million paintings hanging on the walls. And you're dealing with tough and complex corporate issues.

And if you ask me, "Berni, does your wife still love you while you're in there?" my answer is, of course, "Yes she does!"

I mean, I may only be able to give her a fleeting

thought in the middle of all that cut and thrust. But in a split second I can picture her and think of her and the knowledge of her love for me just warms me. You know, I can be cold and lonely, but I just get that sense that tonight I'm going home to my Jacqui.

It's a joy…a delight…to give her a quick call on the mobile phone during a break. Just to hear her voice and connect with her with a quick chat is awesome. It might be only thirty seconds, but out there in the cut and thrust of life I can do that. I can connect with her, even though she doesn't sit in that boardroom with me having that same meeting.

And even if I can't call her, even if I don't have time to think about her for five minutes, I can remember her love in a split second…and it's fantastic! We can be close when we're apart.

Well, it's exactly the same with God. Only God goes one step further. Jacqui can't be with me in that meeting, but God can… and He is. Because that's His promise - a promise I believe with all my heart.

Sometimes if you're a mum changing a dirty nappy and your husband's off at work, he can't be there in the middle of the day when you're dealing with all that stuff, but God can…and God is. God's there.

In the same way that God's sitting with me in that boardroom meeting. In fact, God is one *big* step closer than Jacqui can ever be when I'm not physically with her. He's there in that room. And He's there *in* me! And when I'm sitting in that meeting - and it's tough, and my mind's working at a million miles an hour, and I'm trying to help my clients, and maybe the politics is difficult - in a split second, in just a quick fleeting moment, I can turn my heart towards Christ and just know that He's my Saviour.

Can I tell you…that brings the most incredible, indescribable joy and peace. His Holy Spirit floods over me and fills me. **God is in that place!** And because I am walking in His promises, because I can recall that He's with me, it's awesome! It's a simple faith in Him. Nothing more. Nothing less.

Now, I don't need a mobile phone to talk to God, I can have a quick prayer in an instant with God. Anywhere that I am I can just say, "Ah, thank you Lord! That was awesome!" Or sometimes I'm in a meeting and I can go "Help, God!" or "Lord, I just don't know what to say! What should I say?" And in a split second I feel Him in there with me. His gentle voice speaks in my heart. He guides me this way. Leads me that way.

And whatever your situation is - whether nappies or

business meetings…whatever – God is in that place with you. It's a promise…an unbreakable promise. He will never leave you or forsake you if you have placed your faith in His Son Jesus Christ.

Listen to me…when we start walking in those promises, wow! What a radical transformation in life it is. Something that was once just a distant head knowledge now becomes real. The frustration is gone, because God is in this place.

> AND WHATEVER YOUR SITUATION IS; NAPPIES OR BUSINESS MEETINGS - WHATEVER - GOD IS IN THAT PLACE WITH YOU.

Do you get it? God is in this place…utterly awesome!

Because as we sit in the middle of what we sit in, as we stand in the middle of what we stand in and as we walk in the middle of what we walk in, we can just know that Jesus Christ is with us in every place and circumstance. And He is.

Yes, right there in the cut and thrust of life, we can experience a peace, a joy, a comfort, an intimacy and a help that words simply cannot describe…because God is there.

Not somewhere on the other side of the universe. Not a million miles away. Not down the street and round the corner. Right there where we are. Always.

That's the promise. And to enter this promise, we need only the smallest amount of faith. Not a mountain of faith. Just a mustard seed of faith. That's all it takes to draw close to Jesus…in the middle of life.

CHAPTER FOUR

in that quiet place

in that quiet place

Too Busy to Pray

As we look at how we can draw close to God in the midst of a busy life, it's crucial that we take a look at the whole attitude of, "Well, I'm so busy, I don't have time to pray."

I DON'T HAVE TIME TO PRAY EITHER. HONESTLY, I DON'T.

I can hear you right now. You're thinking, "No, no. You don't understand. I just don't have time." And that's something that - truly - I understand. You see, when I look at my schedule, I don't have time to pray either. Honestly, I don't.

And that's the reality in many people's lives. We decide that we just don't have twenty minutes or half an hour or more each day to pray. And then we wonder why it feels like God's a million miles away.

For much of my life I was too busy for relationships. It's the kind of person that I am.

But when I stepped into the Kingdom of God, what I discovered is that God can do amazing things. Over a period of years, He showed me that in believing the world's "I'm too busy" mantra, I was living a lie…a deception of the enemy. And there came a time when I had to make a decision - to keep feeding myself that lie, or to stop for a reality check and decide to start living in the truth.

I wonder whether it's the same for many other people as well. I know that for many, the reality is that we are busy. It's not everybody's story. But you and I both know that the world is full of distractions. So many things to grab our attention, our thoughts, our time.

In fact, many sociologists contend that whereas a hundred years ago, money was the most valuable thing that people had (for what it could buy), today time is our most valuable commodity. And if that's true, then we'd better make sure we spend it well…for, as the Apostle Paul writes, time is short (1 Corinthians 7:29).

Living in the Promises

Let me take you back to the husband and wife relationship that we talked about earlier. The reason, by the way, that I do that is because the relationship between a husband and wife is the closest and most important relationship that anyone on this earth can have with anyone else on this earth.

If you believe the Bible (and I do), the marriage relationship is a human reflection of the nature of God. You see that time and time again. (Ephesians chapter 5 is just one example). And because it mirrors the nature of God - the deep union between the three Persons of the triune God (Father, Son and Holy Spirit) - it is such a great looking glass back into that nature.

In Chapter One we looked at God's promise that anyone who places their faith in the death and resurrection of Jesus Christ - that is, that Jesus died for them and rose again to pay for their sin - is brought near to God through Christ. So you - who were once far off - are brought near through the blood of Christ (Ephesians 2:13-18).

In Chapter Two we saw how God's desire is to move in with us. The natural next step of a man and woman joining as one through the promise of marriage is that they make a home and a life together, living as one. In effect, living out the promise made at the wedding ceremony. It makes sense when you look at it that way, doesn't it?

And our relationship with God is exactly the same. When we love Him and obey His commandments, He will come and make His home with us. God wants us to live out His promises with Him.

And in the last chapter we saw how we can take those two promises - the promise of being brought close through our faith and the promise of God making His home in us - and actually live them out by connecting with God in the middle of the cut and thrust of the busiest of our days.

We looked at how we can do something about those promises, and live in the promises, and walk in the promises.

But no relationship can get by on a fleeting thought or phone call or SMS message. There's more to an intimate relationship than just that.

Intimacy and Time

It's great that we can connect with God in the middle of a busy day, I do it all the time. But a husband or wife who live their marriage that way will find that their marriage ends in divorce...because we need more than just fleeting interactions, as nice as those are.

Why is that? Well, because a close relationship relies on a deep intimacy - an intimacy that comes from being together, spending time together, without any other people, without any other distractions.

> INTIMACY NEEDS TO BE CONSTANT AND ONGOING BECAUSE IT'S A NATURAL PART OF A LOVING RELATIONSHIP.

As I mentioned earlier, when Jacqui and I were married it was a wonderful wedding. But by far the best part for me was when the car came to pick us up and we left all the people behind...at the reception...and we headed off on our own, because that was our time.

That's when we became husband and wife with no one else around. That's the whole idea of a honeymoon - so you can have intimacy, and rest, and time to be alone and to become husband and wife. It's a time of transition...

from two into one. The two become one. And that takes time.

That's the thing about intimacy - true intimacy.
A one-off... a honeymoon...is not enough.
A honeymoon won't sustain a marriage. Intimacy needs to be constant and ongoing because it's a natural part of a loving relationship between a husband and wife. There's a deep connectedness when a husband and wife experience that emotional and physical intimacy. And it's that deep closeness that we all yearn for.

It's amazing, though, how this world conspires against intimacy... by robbing us of the time that it takes. Somehow, we become convinced, seduced, deluded into thinking that if we chase all those other things out there - like career, status, money and all that stuff we buy and the optimal upbringing for our children...and on and on - that all those things will bring us the satisfaction and significance that we so desperately crave. That's where it's at, surely!

And so those things, little by little, conspire to rob a married couple of time, and therefore of intimacy. "We've just grown apart!" doesn't happen overnight. It happens little by little. And before you know it, this love-struck couple find themselves living different lives. A million miles apart. Because intimacy wasn't a priority in their busy schedule.

The unhurried time together. The coffee… just the two of them… on a Saturday morning. The occasional date. Going out to dinner, or a movie, or even just a walk along the beach.

REAL INTIMACY COMES ONLY WHEN TWO PEOPLE HAVE UNHURRIED TIME TO ENJOY ONE ANOTHER.

The simple things - the things that both of them actually enjoy doing - somehow just slipped off the schedule. Fell by the wayside. Not suddenly. But gradually, over weeks and months and years. An accumulation of time without intimacy.

You see, when intimacy breaks down, then little by little the relationship breaks down. And when the relationship breaks down, intimacy becomes much harder, because the trust on which intimacy depends… evaporates. This whole intimacy and relationship thing are interconnected, because if one of them breaks, it becomes a downward spiral.

Real intimacy comes only when two people have unhurried time to enjoy one another. Can I put it as boldly as this…when they lavish time on one another, the rest of the world might see it as wasting time. Well, okay, then let's waste time on one another. The truth is that what others may see as waste is an investment in intimacy. But it doesn't feel like an investment. It's not a chore - it's an utter delight.

The loss of intimacy leads to a loss of relationship, which in turn feeds and reinforces the loss of intimacy. And if it's true between a husband and wife, it's also true between us and God.

Unhurried Time Alone with God

That's why, when Jesus saw some of the religious leaders - these people who were into public displays of their religiosity, dressed up and praying out loud and, in effect, saying, "Look at me! Look at how super spiritual I am!" - He said, "No, no, no, no! When you pray, go into your room, close the door and pray to your Father in secret. Don't babble a whole bunch of meaningless words and phrases. Pray like this… 'Father, My Father in heaven, hallowed be Your name.'" (my paraphrase - but you can read it for yourself in Matthew 6:1-14)

The radical thing that Jesus did here was calling God *Father*. He actually used the Aramaic word *abba*, which in our language means *dad*.

Dad is a really familiar, loving, respectful term, right? But it was, in fact, heretical for Jesus to refer to God as *Dad*…as *Abba*. The Jews in that day wouldn't even utter the name of God on their lips

DO YOU WANT TO HAVE A CLOSE RELATIONSHIP WITH GOD?

because they held God in such reverence. So for Jesus to come along and say, "Pray like this… 'My Dad in heaven, hallowed be Your name.'"…well, I guess it's no wonder they strung Him up and nailed Him to a Cross!

For Jesus, it wasn't about outward appearances of religiosity, just as a marriage isn't about other people thinking what a lovely couple they make. It was about a very deep, private, intimate time between God and us. That's why He said, "When you pray, go into your room, close the door, and pray to your Father in secret."

Let me be blunt. Do you want to have a close relationship with God? Do you want that awe, that joy, and that peace? Because anyone who wants that kind of a relationship with *Dad*, needs intimate time with Him to share their deepest secrets - the deepest needs of their heart - in a quiet, private place…regularly…every day.

It's not a chore. It's not about wasting time. This is fun. This is intimacy. This is joy. This is peace.

But somehow, just as in marriage, the world seems to have convinced us that this is a waste of time. There are so many other ways to spend our time. So many other priorities. So many other things to do. This notion of unhurried time alone with Jesus…well, it just doesn't fit the world's plan for our lives.

Let me ask you…do you have time to eat? Do you have time to sleep? Do you have time to work? Do you have time to watch TV?

How we spend our time is purely a matter of our priorities.

Finding Time

I have a busy life. So I'm up early in the morning, because I'm at my best at that hour of the day. That's just me. I'm a morning person. I've always been at my best when everyone else is asleep and it's quiet. I'm alert. And for me, it's an awesome time to pray.

Now, that may not work for you. Maybe you have to get up early in the morning and commute to work. Well, Jesus is on that train. Jesus is on that bus. Jesus is in your car. That can be your time where you pray. It's as private as my study in the early morning because no one else knows that you're praying.

Or maybe it's the half hour after the kids go to school. Or, instead of watching that inane half hour show on TV after dinner (doesn't matter how many channels we have, there's never anything decent on!) why not spend it with Jesus? Come on, how many times do we go to the television at night and there's nothing on and yet we watch it anyway?

How many times do people sit there and flick from one channel to the other and waste their time, only because it never occurred to them that they can go and

> WE CAN WASTE TIME WHILE CONVINCING OURSELVES THAT WE JUST DON'T HAVE TIME TO PRAY?

delight themselves in intimate prayer? Do you see how our patterns of behaviour are so entrenched that we can waste time while convincing ourselves that we just don't have time to pray?

Hello?!

The real question is this: How much do you want to experience an intimate relationship with God? How much do want to experience that closeness with God which is His promise to you?

How much?

An Opportunity for You and for Me

Now, before you think I'm pointing my bony finger at you, let me tell you…this is exactly the process that I had to go through to establish a regular time of intimacy with Jesus. We need to get real with ourselves.

And that was difficult for me. I am naturally the sort of person who is more into *doing* than having relationships. I just am. It is so easy for me to get up in the morning, head straight down to the study and check the e-mails that came in from around the world overnight.

> THESE DAYS, THE E-MAILS WAIT UNTIL AFTER I'VE SPENT TIME ALONE WITH JESUS.

Do you know that God convicted me of that one day. I always found that when I checked my e-mails before praying, my mind would wander off and think about what was happening in the ministry in the UK or in Africa.

And God spoke to me about that. So these days, the e-mails wait until *after* I've spent time alone with Jesus. We're human. We are who we are. We have the pressures that we have. That's life.

And that's exactly what robs us of intimacy…in marriage and in our relationship with God.

Jesus said that the most important thing we can do in life is to love the Lord our God with all our heart, with all our soul, with all our mind, and with all our strength. In fact, He said that this is the first and greatest commandment (Matthew 22:37, Mark 12:30, Luke 10:27).

It's the most important thing in life, and it's the thing that Jesus died to give us - an intimate relationship with God. He died so that we could believe in Him and be brought close to God.

Come on! Wake up! How much do you really want to get close to God? If you want to have a close relationship, you have to have intimacy…and intimacy takes time.

And Jesus calls that prayer.

I have never, never, never regretted the time that I've spent in prayer. In fact, what I discovered is that when I first started in regular prayer each day, it felt a bit like a chore. Yet as the days and weeks went by, it's something that I became addicted to.

I long for quiet times with Jesus now. Even though I'm more naturally a 'do-er' than I am a 'pray-er', my times alone with Jesus are such a source of delight. There aren't enough words in the English language to tell you how wonderful it is.

I was having breakfast this morning with some dear friends and we were talking about the ministry. And I said to them, "You know, I love the fact that the Lord's called me to a ministry where I'm able to use the gifts that He's given me. And I have the opportunity to share the good news of Jesus with so many people. I love that!"

But if you gave me a choice between *doing* that ministry, and the quiet times I spend alone with Jesus every day, I would choose those quiet times over the ministry every time.

True! And that's only because those quiet times are so awe inspiring and so beautiful. And that only happened as the relationship grew deeper.

Right now is an opportunity. An opportunity to decide to make those times the *priority* of our lives. Christians go to church and sing songs about putting God first. Songs like *You are exalted above all...*

Well, if time is our most valuable commodity, and if time is limited, who will we spend it on...first?

CHAPTER FIVE

a love letter
from God

CHAPTER FIVE

a love letter from God

Message in a Bottle

We've all seen those movies that start with a message in a bottle. You know…it comes bobbing across the ocean from the other side of the world. And it's washed up on a beach somewhere. And someone comes along and finds the bottle.

And we're all sitting there on the edge of our seats wondering, *"Okay, what does the message say?"* And the music plays and the suspense grows. *"Hurry up!"* we plead. *"Open the bottle and tell us what it says!"*

Now, let me ask you something. If you were the person who found that bottle, what would you do?

Here are your choices:

- (a) You ignore the bottle… *"Sure there's a message in the bottle! So what?!"*

- (b) You pick it up and throw it back into the ocean… *"Let someone else read the stupid message!"*

- (c) You take it home and forget about it… *"I'll get around to it one day!"*

- (d) You open the bottle and read the message… *"I wonder what it says?"*

As Homer Simpson would say, *DOH!*

Obviously we'd pounce on the bottle and open it! Who knows how long it's been in the ocean or where it's come from or who wrote the message or what it says? I mean, how awesome – a message in a bottle!

And what if you opened the bottle and discovered that it was a love letter? A love letter written, in one sense, to anyone. But in another sense, a love letter written specifically to you. Now that would be amazing, wouldn't it?!

As long as people have had ink and paper, there have been love letters.

I mean, love letters…
or cards…or flowers. Love
letters are a really special
way to say, "I love you!"
They say "I love you!" in a
way that nothing else does.
And anybody who has
been through a courtship
will probably have the odd
love letter tucked away
somewhere.

YOU'RE
STRUCK BY THE
OVERWHELMING
INTENSITY OF THE
LOVE OF GOD THAT
OVERFLOWS FROM
EVERY PAGE INTO
YOUR HEART.

There's one love letter, though, that's more special than
any other.

A Special Love Letter

It begins something like this:

*In the beginning God created the heavens and the
earth. Now the earth was formless and empty, darkness
was over the surface of the deep, and the Spirit of God
was hovering over the waters. And God said, "Let
there be light," and there was light. God saw that the
light was good, and he separated the light from the
darkness. God called the light "day," and the darkness he
called "night." And there was evening, and there was
morning – the first day.* (Genesis 1:1-5)

A love letter that begins with an account of where you and I came from. And as you read on, page after page, you're struck by the overwhelming intensity of the love of God that overflows from every page into your heart.

Then a bit further on, somewhere in the middle, it says something like this:

For God so loved the world that he gave his one and only Son, that whoever believes in him shall not perish but have eternal life. For God did not send his Son into the world to condemn the world, but to save the world through him. (John 3:16)

And right towards the end, this is the note…on which the love letter finishes:

Then I saw a new heaven and a new earth, for the first heaven and the first earth had passed away, and there was no longer any sea. I saw the Holy City, the new Jerusalem, coming down out of heaven from God, prepared as a bride beautifully dressed for her husband. And I heard a loud voice from the throne saying, "Now the dwelling of God is with men, and he will live with them. They will be his people, and God himself will be with them and be their God. He will wipe every tear from their eyes. There will be no more death or

> *mourning or crying or pain, for the old order of things has passed away.*" (Revelation 21:1-4)

That is one awesome love letter. And, of course, you will probably recognise that these passages are little chunks out of a huge love letter that, these days, we call the Bible.

Oh No - Not the Bible!

Now, I remember not that many years ago, when people would say "the Bible" and I'd think, "Oh no - not *the Bible!* These old fashioned, irrelevant, Bible-bashing, fundamentalists! How can they even begin to believe in that stuff?! Imagine reading a stuffy old book like that. Really?!"

> THESE OLD FASHIONED, IRRELEVANT, BIBLE-BASHING, FUNDAMENTALISTS! HOW CAN THEY EVEN BEGIN TO BELIEVE IN THAT STUFF?!

But when I read those little bits…and a whole bunch more of the Bible…what I discovered was that it wasn't a fundamentalist religious treatise at all.

Fundamentalism…some dogmatic expression of religion… was never God's idea.

It's something that human beings have taken...and twisted God's love and truth into. When you read the Bible, what you discover is the most awesome love letter, the most amazing plan that God has for your life...and my life...here and now and eternally. It's this huge story of God's engagement of humanity. And in it He reveals His love and grace - a love and a grace that unfolds through the stories of ordinary, fallible people...like you and me.

> I WANT TO SHAKE YOU OUT OF THIS ATTITUDE THAT THE BIBLE IS AN OPTIONAL EXTRA IN OUR WALK WITH GOD.

A story of love and grace that we thought we understood, and then all of a sudden we meet the person of Jesus Christ and realise we understood nothing at all.

Now, I definitely had negative images of the Bible. Absolutely. I just couldn't understand how anybody could even begin to believe that stuff.

You might say, "Berni, that's heresy I believe every word." Well, good for you!

But there are lots of people who say they believe every word, and yet who have one of those thick books at home somewhere on a shelf…or in a cupboard… collecting dust.

Let me get right to the point here. Some people will say, "Why does God seem like He's a million miles away?" But I've found that often they're the same people who have their love letter sitting on a shelf collecting dust.

And my answer is, "He's not. You've just put him on the shelf."

I want to shake you out of this attitude that the Bible is an optional extra in our walk with God. The Bible is alive. It's God's living Word. And when we read it, we need to open it up and say, "Father, I believe this is You talking to me today. I believe this is Your will for my life. I believe that Your Holy Spirit wants to shine Your love and Your light and Your grace and Your wisdom into my heart today through the words on this page."

It's alive. It's the living Word of the living God. It's that message in a bottle. And it's His chosen way of speaking with us. Not through some dry, theological text, but through real life stories that engage our hearts and captivate us with His awesome love.

What an Amazing Book

The Bible was written over a 1500 year period, starting

around about 1350 BC and finishing towards the end of the first century AD. It was written (originally) in three different languages - Hebrew, Aramaic, and Greek. It has many different authors from different cultures, in different time periods, and with different backgrounds... with different things going on when the 66 different books of the Bible were written.

The Bible's been translated into hundreds of languages. And, you know something? It's been copied by hand. Because before the invention of Gutenberg's printing press in the mid 1400's, there was no other way of replicating the Bible. The only way to create copies of the Bible back then was for people called scribes to write the whole thing out, by hand, over and over and over again. Can you believe that?

The scholars, the historians, and the 'textual critics' will agree that there are very, very few transcription errors in this Book. That's because a whole bunch of experts have pieced together the historical trails of handwritten manuscripts of the original texts (of which there are literally thousands), compared them, picked up any minor errors that crept in, and corrected them.

There are a handful of uncertain words in some non-critical passages, but - by and large - the Bible that we read today contains precisely the words that were written back then. God has gone to a lot of trouble to preserve this God-inspired book - His love letter to us. In fact, in historical terms it is the most accurate and well-attested-to historical document that we have from antiquity - by a country mile. It's the story of God. It's the story of who God is, what His plan is, who we are in Jesus Christ and how we can respond to His great love.

It's this vast, amazing, profound love letter personally guided down though the waves and oceans of time over the past 3,500 years. And like a message in a bottle, like a love letter, it is now placed in our hands. It's placed in your hands. And it's placed in my hands.

> IN HISTORICAL TERMS IT IS THE MOST ACCURATE AND WELL-ATTESTED-TO HISTORICAL DOCUMENT THAT WE HAVE FROM ANTIQUITY.

Everything But…

Now, I know that there are going to be some people who read this book who get to this point and think to themselves, "You know something? Chapters One to Four? No problem. I love what he said in those chapters. And I want to live my life like that. But Chapter Five? I have a problem with that chapter. What I'm going to do is I'm going to live out Chapters One to Four. But just quietly…I'm going to give Chapter Five a miss."

In other words, "I want to be close to God…and I want everything but the Bible. It's hard to read. It doesn't all make sense. No…I just can't do that bit."

And just between you and me, that's where I started out. Even when I was at 'Bible' college studying a degree in this stuff, there was still a little bit of that swilling around inside me. And it took a man of God, a man who I admire so much - Dr Barry Chant, the Principal of the college - to deal with that attitude in me.

Here's the story. I was a busy businessman and I attended Bible college part time. One of the subjects which I had to complete was essentially a subject on how to preach. And we would sit around each week listening to each other preach. I thought it was such a waste of time. I was a good communicator. I'd travelled around the world speaking at large IT conferences in my business career.

So after a few weeks I asked Barry to give me a credit for this subject…so that I could be excused from this thing that was wasting my time. On the surface, it was an entirely reasonable request. But something in the wise spirit of this man - a man who'd been walking with the

Lord for over half a century - caused him to shake his head. "No, I still want to hear you preach a couple more times" he said.

I was infuriated with the man.

So the next time I preached, his critique went something like this… "*Berni, you're a great communicator. You know something though? When you preach, you stray too far away from God's Word. You tell us what you think instead of what God is saying. You need to bring people back to the Bible, back to God's Word. Because it's God's Word that transforms people's lives, not your wisdom.*"

That hurt. My pride smarted at the criticism. But you know something? He was spot on. After that, he let me go. And since that time, millions of people have benefited from his wisdom, because it's a lesson that's stuck with me ever since.

Have a look at what Peter the apostle says:

> *For you have been born again, not of perishable seed, but of imperishable, through the living and enduring word of God. For, "All men are like grass, and all their glory is like the flowers of the field; the grass withers and the flowers fall, but the word of the Lord stands forever." And this is the word that was preached to you.* (1 Peter 1:23-25)

The things that happen to us here on earth…they come and go. They're temporary. But God's Word stands forever. God's Word is God speaking to us of His love. God and God's Word are inseparable.

> HOW DO WE IMAGINE THAT WE CAN EVER BE CLOSE TO HIM WITHOUT LISTENING TO HIM?

God's Word is God speaking. How do we imagine that we can ever be close to Him without listening to Him?

We men would love to think that we can be close to our wives without listening to what they have to say. I once saw a cartoon…it was a drawing of a man's ear, and it had a hearing aid in it. There were two settings on the hearing aid – 'ON' and 'WIFE'!

But as any wife will tell you, there can be no intimacy without deep communication. And that involves listening.

God's principal chosen means of speaking to you and me is through His Word - the Bible. Leave that in the cupboard and we can forget about drawing close to God.

"Everything but…" is not enough. Because God's Word is not some transient thing like our feelings or our circumstances. It stands forever. It will never fail. It is the truth, whether the world receives it or not.

So often you hear people quote a piece of Scripture that goes something like this:

> *"The truth will set you free."* (John 8:32)

But that's only half of what Jesus said, and a half truth is nothing more than a lie. The devil himself is very good at quoting God's Word out of context and twisting it into a lie.

Here's the whole thing:

> *"You will know the truth and the truth will set you free."* (John 8:32)

In other words, in order for the truth to set you free, you have to *know* it.

My life has been utterly transformed by God. And it goes on being transformed. And as I have often shared with people, the biggest thing that God ever set me free from was...me. And that's something that He's still doing.

Now, I would love to tell you that He did that because I took to heart what I shared with you in the first four chapters of this book. And I know that you would love me to nudge you, wink my eye, and whisper quietly, "Don't worry about Chapter Five. It doesn't really matter. Stick to the first four and you'll be right!"

I know that. But if I did that, it would only be half the truth…and that's nothing more than a lie. You and I can't be over *here*, and leave the truth over *there* in a cupboard - or on a shelf somewhere gathering dust - and expect it somehow, mysteriously to set us free.

It don't work that way!

> UNLESS I HAD SPENT TIME READING HIS WORD OVER THESE LAST YEARS, I SIMPLY WOULD NOT HAVE THE INTIMATE RELATIONSHIP WITH GOD THAT I NOW ENJOY.

To be completely honest with you, the time that I have spent listening to the voice of God through the Word of God has utterly transformed my life. It has brought me near, as He has written His Word through His Spirit on my heart.

And what's more, just like the time of prayer, reading and meditating on His Word is the great joy of my life. In fact, it's an integral part of those quiet times alone with Jesus. It's not a chore, but a joy and a delight.

It does not overstate the matter to say that unless I had spent time reading His Word over these last years, I simply would not have the intimate relationship with God that I now enjoy.

And I fully expect that as the months and years roll on, and I continue in that daily habit of reading and meditating on His Word, the intimacy of that relationship will grow ever richer and deeper, until one day I'll stand before Him and see Him in all His glory.

Just Do It

I'll say it again…God has gone to an enormous amount of trouble to preserve His love letter for you and me, here and now, today. That's why the excuse, "I'm just too busy to read the Bible!" is so feeble. Do you see how inappropriate that is? No wonder it feels like God is a million miles away!

All the time, He just wants to speak His promises into our hearts, whisper His love into our ears, and breathe His grace into our lives. And the one principal way that He has chosen to do that is through His love letter - the Bible.

How can we be too busy?

God has brought us near through faith in Jesus Christ.

He has set up His home in us through his Holy Spirit. God is with us in every moment of every day, right through the cut and thrust of life. He calls us into an intimate relationship with Him. And God has written a love letter to us. That love letter is called the Bible. And He would speak to us every day through His Word…if only we would listen.

God *is* here in this place with you and me. Right here.

And through the Cross of Christ, He is crying out to you and to me:

"Come. Come and be close to Me."

On a Personal Note

It's so easy to come to the end of this book and be both excited and discouraged. Excited at the prospect of forging a new, intimate relationship with God. Discouraged because…well, *"It all seems so daunting,"* you might think *"I mean, this guy writing this book makes it sound so simple. But all these years, God has seemed so far away."*

And it would be daunting, if it were all up to us. But it isn't. Because far from being some passive player, deep in His mighty heart God yearns for us. He yearns so deeply and so mightily that we cannot begin to comprehend how much He wants to be close to us.

And all it takes is for us to take the first step. A step of faith to believe. A step of spending quiet time alone with Him. A step of immersing ourselves in His love letter to us.

Change is always daunting. And no doubt the devil would sit on our shoulders and whisper words of doubt into our minds. The enemy wants nothing more than to divert us from this pursuit of God. To set us off course, so that we miss the mark. (That's literally what the word *sin* means - to miss the mark. To miss the point.)

But the prize - this intimate closeness with God - is without equal. There is nothing like it on earth. Or in the heavens, for that matter. When the Spirit of God fills us to overflowing, when we experience God for ourselves, in His Word, through His Spirit, in our quite times and in our hectic times - it leaves us utterly changed.

Longing for more.

Let us not pretend that this is some chore - a chore of learning and dissecting and putting our understanding of God in neat little piles of theology. Don't get me wrong...I'm passionate about studying theology. And I would encourage you, if you haven't already, to take a step down that path.

But right now I'm talking simply about drawing close to this infinite God - a God who is so vast, so deep, so rich, so gracious, so merciful, so loving, so utterly wondrous and mysterious and knowable all at the same time, that His very nature defies any attempt by us to dissect Him into a trite little set of doctrines. I am not talking about that at all.

My prayer for you is that by faith, with the desire of the Spirit burning in your heart, that you would immerse yourself in God Himself. That this oneness that Jesus talked about so much, this intimacy that He purchased for you and me on the Cross, would be something that you desire with every fibre of your being. And that as the days and weeks and months and years slip by, you will know the great delight of looking back on those times and seeing how God has honoured your desire and your faltering first steps.

He's not looking for perfection today. We look and judge on the outside. But God…God looks on our hearts. And as He looks on our hearts today - yours and mine - may He see a spark of desire that He Himself will fan into a raging fire by His Spirit.

May you know your God more deeply than you ever thought possible…by the grace of Jesus Christ.

Berni Dymet

christianity**works**.com

Our passion here at Christianityworks is leading millions of people, one by one, into a dynamic relationship with Jesus as we proclaim the Gospel through the media around the globe.

That's something that we do each and every day through Christianityworks' radio and television broadcasts, in over 160 countries.

And of course through the internet.

christianityworks.com is jam packed full of teaching resources, free downloads and eBooklets and much, much more.

So check it out for yourself – on your computer, tablet or smartphone.

eDevotional.net

Receive words of inspiration, hope and encouragement from Berni Dymet - delivered daily right into your in box.

To live each day in victory, we know that we need to connect with God through His Word. But all too often, we seem too busy to open the Bible.

Well, that's where *A Different Perspective* – Berni Dymet's Daily eDevotional – can help you.

A Scripture verse, a few words of encouragement and a 60 second audio message delivered to your mobile, tablet or computer each weekday.

Go to eDevotional.net and complete the form for *instant access*.

It's completely free, because Berni just wants to help you win your daily battles – each and every day!

And when you do subscribe, we'll also bless you with a FREE GIFT - by sending you Berni's powerful eBook: *How to Get Close to God.*

So, what are you waiting for?

Be blessed through your daily eDevotional from Berni ... at **eDevotional.net**

My Gift to Keep Christianityworks on Air Around the Globe

Yes! I want play my part in sharing the love of Jesus with millions of people through the media.

My gift: £_____

(Tax deductible in Australia)

Title: _____

First Name: _____

Surname: _____

Address: _____

Town/Suburb: _____

Postcode: _____ State: _____

Phone: _____

Email: _____

Please see over for Giving Details...

UK: PO Box 201 | Chessington | KT9 9BX | 0800 078 6565
Australia: PO Box 1729 | Bondi Junction | NSW | 1355 | 1300 722 415
India: PO Box 1602 | Secunderabad | 500 003 | Telangana

Giving Details:

☐ **I've enclosed my cheque/money order made out to Christianityworks**

☐ **Please Debit my Credit Card**

  ☐ This is a one-time gift

  ☐ I would like to make an ongoing monthly gift

  ☐ Visa ☐ MasterCard ☐ AMEX

Card Number:

☐☐☐☐ ☐☐☐☐ ☐☐☐☐ ☐☐☐☐

Security No. (CVV)

☐☐☐☐ (3 or 4 digit)

Name on Card:

Expiry Date:

☐☐ / ☐☐

Signature: **Date:**

Please return this form with your gift of support to christianityworks in the envelope provided.

you can Give securely online at 🖱
christianityworks.com

For direct deposits our account details are:
Name: Good News Broadcasting
BSB: 062 246
Acct no: 1012 7204